The
Boy with the
FASTER
BRAIN

by
Peter Shankman

The Boy with the Faster Brain
© 2023 by Peter Shankman

ISBN 979-8-9877036-0-1 paperback
ISBN 979-8-9877036-1-8 ebook

Illustrations: Isabela Flores de Moura
Book Design: Carla Green, Clarity Designworks

$$x = \frac{-b \pm \sqrt{b^2 - 4a.c}}{2.a}$$

This book is dedicated to my daughter, Jessa. I believe that there's nothing in the world you can't do. You continue to amaze me every single day, and not a day goes by where you don't make me want to be better version of myself. I love you with everything I am, and will always be there for you.

Introduction

A note to parents: When I wrote *Faster Than Normal* in 2017, it immediately changed the conversation we have around ADHD and all forms of Neurodiversity, and it did so beyond my wildest dreams. As a child growing up in the 70s and 80s in the Public School system of New York City, ADHD didn't exist. What did exist was "sit down, Peter, you're disrupting the class," and that was a refrain I heard almost every single day from kindergarten through high school. I wasn't diagnosed with ADHD until my mid 30s, and by then, I'd already started and sold two companies, and was about to launch my third. It was at that moment that I realized that all the trouble I'd gotten into, all the days I came home crying after being labeled "different," was the absolute best thing I could ever have hoped to happen to me.

I promise you, whether you can see it now or not, your child having a neurodiverse brain is quite possibly the greatest gift they'll ever get. Once they learn how to "drive" their faster than normal brain, the possibilities for them are, simply put, unlimited. What your children will be able to do with their lightning fast speed and gifts will shock you. I speak from experience—My parents are still shocked daily by what I've done, and I'm 50 years old!

Talk to your children. Explain that there's absolutely nothing wrong with them. Show them that they're about to learn how to drive the race car that is their brain, and once they do, they'll be faster than everyone else. Your children aren't broken, they're gifted, and I swear to you: They're going to change the world.

I want to hear from you, by the way. My email is peter@shankman.com, and I'm @petershankman on all of the socials. I encourage you to reach out to me. The more we continue to shine light on neurodiversity and mental health, the better our society will be for it.

Acknowledgements
Thank yous are due to my wonderful parents, Nancy and Ira, my assistant Meagan Murphy, David, Kira, Jen, as well as every guest of the Faster Than Normal podcast who have taught me so much and been so generous with their knowledge.

Lastly, this book wouldn't have ever happened without my life partner, Gabriella. Gab, you bring out the best in me, no matter what I'm doing, and I only hope I do the same for you. I'm blessed to have you in my life. May our travels together throughout our days continue to take us around the world and back, over and over again. I love you.

"AGAIN?!"

Peter's mom wasn't happy when he came home with a note from his teacher for the fourth time in two weeks.

Peter watched his mom unseal the envelope, pull out the note and read it to herself, her eyebrows getting more and more crunched up with every line.

"I'm grounded again, aren't I," asked Peter.

"Go upstairs and start your homework," his mom said. "We'll talk about it when your father gets home."

Peter took out his school books and started to do his math homework. But as usual, he stopped after the first few problems and started thinking about other things. This time, he was thinking about his day, and what he did to get into trouble in class.

The teacher had asked the class a question having to do with history. Peter knew the right answer, but instead of giving it to the teacher, he raised his hand, and when he was called on, he made a joke. The entire class laughed, but Peter, even though he knew he did something wrong, felt like he just got stuck by a bolt of lightning! The class laughing at his joke somehow gave him energy!

Unfortunately for Peter, he had to use that energy to march down to the principal's office and get his punishment for talking out in class.

Peter was jolted back to reality by the sound of the front door opening. He knew his dad was home from work, and he knew he was about to get in serious trouble. He imagined his mom showing his dad the note and them both marching upstairs to take away his computer, his iPad, and his TV.

"Clomp, clomp, clomp!" Peter heard his parents' footsteps on the stairs outside his room. He got ready for the worst.

"Hey, Champ," said his dad, as he and Peter's mom entered his bedroom. "Tough day at school?"

"Yeah, I guess so," said Peter, looking down at his shoes. He hated disappointing his parents, especially after he'd promised so many times to work harder and not make jokes in class.

"Peter, what happens when you make those jokes in school," asked his dad.

"I get in trouble," Peter said.

"Well yeah," said his dad. "But what else? What happens to you? What happens inside your head?"

Peter paused and thought. Finally, he answered: "I know I shouldn't make jokes in class, but when I do, I feel like, really powerful. When the other kids laugh, it's almost like they're giving me some of their energy so I can focus on the work and not get distracted," Peter said."

"I guess," sighed Peter sadly, "that doesn't make any sense, huh?"

"Actually, Peter," said his dad, "it makes perfect sense. You see, my brain works the same way."

"IT DOES?" asked Peter, incredulously.

"Yup. It does," said his dad. "And here's what we're gonna do about it."

As they sat at dinner eating their hamburgers, Peter's dad told Peter a story:

"When I was a young boy, Peter, I got into trouble, just like you. My teachers told me to 'sit still,' and to 'stop disrupting the class.' School was really tough for me, just like it is for you."

"What did you do about it, Dad?" asked Peter.

"Well, back then, there wasn't much to do. I managed to finish school, but it wasn't until I was an adult that I finally realized why I was different. You see, Peter, our brains are a little different than everyone else. You could say that our brains are faster than normal."

Peter looked confused: "Faster than normal? What does that mean?"

"Well, it means that we think faster than other people. And because of that, sometimes we say things without thinking—kind of like what you did in class today. It's like our brains don't really hear the part of us that says 'maybe we shouldn't say that…' And before we know it, we've said it, and then we get in trouble. You know what I mean?"

Peter nodded enthusiastically. He certainly did.

His dad continued: "Sometimes, our brains go so fast that we stop paying attention to what we're supposed to be focusing on, and we get distracted. That happens to you a lot, right?"

Peter nodded.

"Well, the key is to figure out how to use our brains the best way we can. Think about a super-fast sports car. If you don't know how to drive it and you press all the way down on the gas pedal, what do you think will happen?"

"You'll crash! Boom!" exclaimed Peter.

"Correct," said his dad. "But what happens if you take lessons and learn how to drive that super-fast car?"

Peter thought for a second. "I guess you'd become a great race car driver?"

"Correct again! You just need to learn how to drive your faster brain," said his dad.

"But how can I learn that?" asked Peter. "Everything I've tried so far hasn't worked!"

"Don't worry," said his mom, smiling. "We've got an idea for you. Now finish your dinner so you can get to the rest of your homework."

The next day, Peter's mom surprised Peter by picking him up from school. "We're going to visit with a special doctor today, Peter!"

Peter was nervous. He asked his mom, "Will I have to get a shot?"

His mom smiled. "No, honey. It's not that kind of doctor. This is more of a… Feelings doctor. Her name is Doctor Lisa, and you're just going to talk with her."

"This doesn't look like any doctor's office I've ever seen before," Peter said when he and his mom first walked in. "Mom, there are video games here! And VR glasses! Ooh! Can I play with the VR glasses?"

"Let's see what Dr. Lisa says first," Peter's mom said.

Right at that moment, Dr. Lisa walked into the waiting room. She was dressed in blue jeans, and Peter thought she looked more like a teacher in his school than a doctor.

"Hey there," Dr. Lisa exclaimed with a huge, welcoming smile. "You must be Peter and Peter's mom!"

"That's me," said Peter, adding "can I play with the VR headset?"

"Let's talk first, then I'll challenge you to a game of 'Beat Saber.' How's that sound?"

"You play Beat Saber?" Peter asked, amazed.

"I do, and I'm pretty good at it," said Dr. Lisa. "How about you and I go inside and talk? Your mom can wait here if she wants."

"OK! Bye mom!" said Peter.

Dr. Lisa's office was even cooler than the waiting room, with rock and roll posters and cool graffiti all over the walls. As Peter sat down, Dr. Lisa gave Peter a fidget spinner to play with.

"Peter, your mom tells me that school is a little tough for you sometimes. I want to learn more about that from you. Tell me more about what happens in school."

"I guess. I mean, I love school, and I really like some of the stuff I'm learning. But sometimes… I dunno. I guess I zone out a bit. Sometimes it gets really hard to concentrate, and I want to do other things. I'll start daydreaming, or I'll think of something funny and want to share it with my friends. I know I shouldn't, but sometimes I can't help myself, and that's why I get in trouble. I guess I'm just not a good kid." Peter's voice got quiet, he felt his face turning red, and he felt himself trying really hard not to cry.

"Peter, there's nothing wrong with you," said Dr. Lisa. "I want you to know that right away. You're not a bad kid, and you're not a bad student. That much I'm sure of. It sounds, though, like there are some things that you struggle with at school and we're going to work together to help with that. Now, tell me about the stuff in school you love."

Peter's face lit up. "I love science! I love learning about technology. In our tech class we're learning about computers, and my teacher tells me that I'm the quickest learner he's ever had! He even lets me help fix other kids' problems when their computers aren't working!"

"What do you think is different about you when you're in your tech class versus when you're in, say, social studies?"

"Maybe I love tech so much that I don't have time to daydream," Peter asked.

Dr. Lisa smiled. "Exactly, Peter. Our brains are amazing things and capable of helping us in SO many ways. When our brain sees that we love what we're doing, it lets us focus really well on that thing. When we're doing something we don't love as much, or aren't as interested in, our brain has to work harder, but it helps us by making certain chemicals that help us focus.

"Your brain moves much faster than a regular brain, Peter. If your brain was a spaceship, you'd be cruising at Warp 9 most of the time."

Peter interrupted: "Like in Star Trek!"

"Exactly," said Dr. Lisa. "But because your brain moves so fast, sometimes it gets a little bored. If you happen to be working on something that doesn't excite you as much as tech class, for instance, your brain might start telling you that it needs some help focusing. Sometimes, without even knowing it, your brain tells you to do things like make jokes, or daydream, because it's actually trying to focus on what you're learning!"

Peter was confused: "if my brain wants me to focus, why would it make me daydream or interrupt the class with a joke?"

"Great question, Peter," said Dr. Lisa. "We're going to work together to learn why your brain does that, and more importantly, what we can do to give your brain what it needs, without you doing anything that could get you in trouble. How does that sound?"

"That sounds great, Dr. Lisa! Can we play Beat Saber now?"

Dr. Lisa smiled. "Absolutely."

Over the next several months, Peter met Dr. Lisa every week to learn how to "drive" his faster brain. He learned about other ways of giving his brain those chemicals it needed so he could focus on his work, instead of making jokes or talking out of turn in class. He learned how movement and exercise, like running around and playing before school started could help him drive his brain.

Dr. Lisa talked to Peter's teachers and explained how his brain worked, and together, they mapped out a plan for Peter. Now, when Peter starts to get distracted in class, instead of making a joke or interrupting the lesson, Peter quietly gets up and walks to the back of the room. Simply by getting up and standing for a little while, he's able to control his brain better.

Dr. Lisa also taught Peter "cognitive behavioral therapy" (but Peter just calls it CBT), which is a cool way of learning how to change certain things about the way your brain works. It was really easy for Peter to learn, and more than that, it was fun!

Peter also learned about mindfulness and breathing exercises. Peter never thought he could learn to breathe, he just assumed that was something he did all the time anyway. But by learning to focus on his breathing when he wanted to speak out, he was able to channel his faster brain in better directions.

As time passed, Peter started to realize when he was getting bored, and could do the things he needed to do to keep his brain working and on track. In fact, towards the end of the school year, Peter came home again with a note from his teacher, the first one in a long time.

"Uh oh," said Peter's mom and dad, who were both home when Peter walked in. "What happened?"

"You should just read it," said Peter, trying hard not to smile.

> *"Dear Peter's parents: I just want to let you know that Peter got the highest grade on today's test of any student in the class. He's an entirely different student than he was at the beginning of the year. He's a pleasure to have in class, he participates actively, he doesn't interrupt, he listens and is clearly thinking before he speaks.*
>
> *You should both be very proud of how far Peter has come and the vast amount of improvement he's shown this year. Congratulations to him!"*

Peter's mom and dad couldn't stop smiling. They were so proud of Peter! And Peter was pretty proud of himself, too!

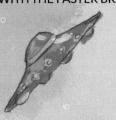

Resources

Peter's Mailing List: shank.mn/emails

The Faster Than Normal Podcast:
fasterthannormal.com

CHADD: chadd.org

Contact Peter: peter@shankman.com

Made in the USA
Las Vegas, NV
21 March 2024